K-Pop

Other titles in the *Music Scene* series include:

Country Music

EDM

Pop Music

Rap and Hip-Hop

K-Pop

Stuart A. Kallen

San Diego, CA

© 2020 ReferencePoint Press, Inc.
Printed in the United States

For more information, contact:
ReferencePoint Press, Inc.
PO Box 27779
San Diego, CA 92198
www.ReferencePointPress.com

LIBRARY OF CONGRESS CATALOGING-IN-PUBLICATION DATA

Names: Kallen, Stuart A., 1955– author.
Title: K-Pop/by Stuart A. Kallen.
Description: San Diego, CA: ReferencePoint Press, [2019] | Series: Music
 Scene | Includes bibliographical references and index.
Identifiers: LCCN 2019019704 (print) | LCCN 2019019988 (ebook) | ISBN
 9781682826447 (eBook) | ISBN 9781682826430 (hardback)
Subjects: LCSH: Popular music—Korea (South)—History and
 criticism—Juvenile literature.
Classification: LCC ML3502.K6 (ebook) | LCC ML3502.K6 K35 2019 (print) | DDC
 781.63095195—dc23
LC record available at https://lccn.loc.gov/2019019704

CONTENTS

INTRODUCTION

A Worldwide Explosion

In June 2018 over fifty-three thousand K-pop fans attended KCON, the South Korean pop music convention held in Newark, New Jersey. American devotees of K-pop shrieked, shouted, and sang along to Korean songs performed by beloved K-pop bands like Exo, Super Junior, and BTS. Music journalist Amy X. Wang describes the Exo concert in the following way: "Several thousand people are screaming their hearts out in a language they don't speak."[1]

But knowing Korean is not crucial for under-standing the catchy melodies, stellar vocal harmo-nies, and popping popcorn beats that fans adore. K-pop songs feature a dizzying array of sounds that mix dubstep beats, rapid-fire Korean rap, ex-otic Asian melodies, sweeping electronic dance synthesizers, and pop rock sing-alongs. As Wang puts it, "By mashing together genres and cultures, K-pop songs kick the familiar rhythms of American pop music up a notch."[2]

The musical complexities of K-pop groups are further celebrated in their high-drama, stylized mu-sic videos. These videos have been compared to mini movies that have elaborate storylines about ro-mance, heartbreak, betrayal, dreams, nightmares, time travel, and even murder. As the plots unfold, teenage heartthrobs perform intricate moves choreographed by some of the best dancers in the world.

Giving Fans a Voice

The feast of the senses presented in K-pop music and videos has attracted tens of millions of young fans in the United States, Canada, Asia, and Europe. Twenty-three million such fans can be found on the English-language website Soompi, which covers South Korean popular culture. Soompi community manager Kristine Ortiz explains K-pop's attraction for its many fans: "It's a process of self-discovery and that makes it really exciting," she says. "Users find one song and they start digging on their own. There's a level of motivation and socializing you don't see with [other] artists."[3] Ortiz says some Western fans even learn Korean so they can keep up with the K-pop scene.

> "By mashing together genres and cultures, K-pop songs kick the familiar rhythms of American pop music up a notch."[2]
>
> —Amy X. Wang, music journalist

K-pop band Exo performs in 2014. K-pop songs feature a dizzying array of sounds that mix dubstep beats, rapid-fire Korean rap, exotic Asian melodies, electronic rhythms, and pop rock sing-alongs.

Because it is such an engaging and engrossing genre of music, K-pop fans work tirelessly on social media to promote their favorite acts. Online forums dedicated to K-pop are abuzz with fans translating lyrics, analyzing the latest extravagant video, and gossiping about the love lives of their favorite K-pop stars, who are adoringly referred to as idols. This in part explains why, in 2018, the audio streaming platform Spotify reported that K-pop tracks were streamed more than 14 billion times globally, making it one of the most popular musical genres in the world. In addition, the streaming station Pandora reported "Fake Love" by BTS was streamed more than 175 million times in 2018. Songwriter, DJ, and music producer Steve Aoki explains the importance of these numbers: "With streaming, fans now have such a large voice, and that's how BTS really became a phenomenon—because the fans made it a phenomenon."[4]

K-Pop Is Here to Stay

Driven by its enthusiastic fans, K-pop has swelled to a global industry worth more than $5 billion. And as the sound melds with mainstream pop culture worldwide, K-pop is consistently shattering music industry records. K-pop idols are receiving more views on YouTube, getting more streams on Spotify, and climbing up the *Billboard* Hot 100 pop charts faster than any other musical superstars.

K-pop bands like BlackPink, GOT7, and BTS are providing strong competition for established artists like Justin Bieber, Taylor Swift, and Ed Sheeran. With unshakeable hooks, eye-popping outfits, and expert choreography, K-pop's fusion of Eastern and Western music, fashion, and dance is destined to be around for a long time. As music journalist Brian O'Flynn writes, "K-pop isn't going anywhere. . . . As this cultural phenomenon continues to balloon, you better get into it, or get out of [the] way."[5]

CHAPTER ONE

Origins of K-Pop

Around 50 million people live in South Korea, which is about the size of Indiana. Most Americans had never heard music produced in the nation until 2012, when the singer, rapper, and dancer known as Psy released a video of his hit song "Gangnam Style." At the time, Psy was little known outside of South Korea. However, the "Gangnam Style" video, with its catchy electronic beats and amusing horse-riding dance moves, struck a universal chord. Within weeks, "Gangnam Style" became a worldwide sensation, and by the end of the year, it had become the first video on YouTube ever to have been viewed 1 billion times. The song went on to top the charts in more than thirty countries, including Australia, the United Kingdom, France, Russia, Spain, and Canada.

The Godfather of K-Pop

Psy might have been the face that introduced the United States to Korean popular music, but the roots of K-pop can be traced back decades to American music and the music television channel MTV. The songs and videos topping the US charts in the 1980s strongly influenced a South

Korean record producer few Americans had ever heard of— Lee Soo-man. Lee is considered the godfather of K-pop today, but he began his career in 1972 as a guitar-strumming folk-singer in Seoul, the capital of South Korea. By 1980, however, Lee's tastes had changed. Influenced by Western rock groups like Led Zeppelin and Black Sabbath, he formed a heavy metal band called Lee Soo Man and 365 Days. The band featured loud, distorted guitars, extended bass and drum solos, and screamed vocals.

South Korean pop star Psy performs in New York in 2013. Most Americans had never heard music produced in South Korea until 2012, when Psy released a video of his hit song "Gangnam Style."

Lee's heavy metal sound was unique in South Korea, but it was unappreciated. At the time, the country's authoritarian government strictly censored entertainers and the media. Lee's music was banned from the airwaves. In 1981 Lee decided there was no future in the South Korean entertainment business. He moved to Southern California to attend college.

Lee was living in the United States when MTV went on the air on August 1, 1981. The channel introduced the world to fast-paced music videos featuring colorfully dressed musicians singing and dancing their way through three-minute songs. By 1985 MTV had ushered in a new era, reshaping tastes in music, video, and fashion. Lee returned home with a plan to introduce South Korea to the flashy dance moves and slick pop music he had seen on American television.

To this end, in 1988 Lee founded SM Studio (later referred to as SM Entertainment, or SME), a music recording studio and artist management business. Lee's timing seemed perfect. Seoul was hosting the Summer Olympics that year, which focused international attention on South Korean pop culture, known as *Hallyu*, or Korean Wave. Hallyu includes South Korean movies and dramatic TV shows called K-dramas. Korean comics (*manhwa*), and animated films (*aeni*) are also Hallyu, as are Korean foods like grilled meat bulgogi and the spicy cabbage dish kimchi. The late 1980s also saw the South Korean government relax its censorship practices. This allowed the nation's singers, songwriters, and musicians to freely express themselves.

Culture Technology, K-Pop Hit Maker

Lee tried to take advantage of South Korea's new musical freedom, but his new studio was nearly destroyed the same year it opened when heavy rains flooded the control room. Rather than quit, Lee began working as a DJ so he could save enough money to buy new microphones, digital recorders, computers, and keyboard synthesizers.

While spinning records in dance clubs, Lee studied his audiences. He began to pay attention to which types of electronic dance music (EDM) made people dance and which songs made them wander off to the bar. Back in his studio, Lee worked to create music that sounded like the most popular club songs that got the most people dancing. He expanded his knowledge by hiring classically trained songwriters and students of electronic music.

By 1990 Lee was searching South Korean bars and theaters for talent, and that is how he found his first K-pop idol. Nineteen-year-old Hyun Jin-young was a thin male singer with a high, girlish voice. Lee taught Hyun to rap and dance and dressed him in baggy clothes like those worn by American hip-hop artists. The formula proved to be a success. Hyun's 1993 debut album, *IWBH*, short for *International World Beat and Hip-Hop*, sold over four hundred thousand copies. However, Hyun's success was brief. He was arrested for smoking marijuana, which is considered a major crime in South Korea. Hyun's dramatic fall was as fast as his rise to stardom.

Lee learned a lot from the experience: he decided that in the future, he would develop numerous acts, rather than pour all his time and money into developing a single star. This insight guided Lee when he launched Culture Technology, a star-production system created to train a reliable roster of K-pop performers. In 1995 Lee conducted a worldwide talent search, sending out scouts to audition songwriters, singers, and dancers in South Korea, Japan, and the United States. Because of his previous success with *IWBH*, Lee's auditions attracted a large number of talented young performers who hoped to be the next Hyun. Most of those recruited as performers were middle school or high school students. Recruits who passed their auditions quit school, signed contracts with SME, and moved to Seoul for training.

The Culture Technology process created by Lee is very rigorous and extremely competitive. It has changed little over the years,

Life of a K-Pop Trainee

Life can be difficult for K-pop trainees who are recruited by large music-production companies like SM Entertainment. Looks are just as important as talent, and recruits are put on strict diets to maintain thin figures and good complexions. Some are required to undergo painful cosmetic surgery procedures to make their eyes, jaw, nose, and forehead look more like elfin anime characters. Trainees also use creams and bleaches to whiten their skin. For all their painstaking sacrifices, there is no guarantee that a trainee will be a K-pop star. Prospective idols regularly perform for judges who are merciless when pointing out weaknesses. Those who do not live up to the high production standards are fired.

Life does not improve much for those who go on to debut as K-pop performers. Successful trainees are required to pay back the entertainment company by working as pop idols. Most receive minimum wage, whereas the producers bring in millions from record sales, concert appearances, merchandise sales, and product endorsements. In addition, one's career can be short; fans constantly expect idols to outdo themselves, and those who fail to deliver are quickly forgotten. As dancer and choreographer Ellen Kim explains, "Korean people want something new every week, and . . . that's the hardest pressure, probably. To come up with something catchy all the time, a hit all the time, and you've got tons of artists and the lifespan of one song is so short."

Quoted in Joseph L. Flatley, "K-Pop Takes America: How South Korea's Music Machine Is Conquering the World," Verge, October 18, 2012. www.theverge.com.

remains in place today, and has been adopted by other K-pop production companies. For a chance at becoming a K-pop star, trainees, most of whom are ages ten to sixteen, leave their friends and families behind. They give up their personal lives and most belongings, including computers and cell phones (except on weekends). Trainees move into company dormitories, where the entertainment company pays for all living expenses, including food and clothing. Tutors are hired so recruits can continue with their education.

K-pop hopefuls spend their days and nights in a regimented, structured learning environment overseen by managers and trainers. They practice singing, dancing, acting, and speaking English, Japanese, Mandarin, and other languages. Suk-Young Kim, professor of performance studies at the University of California, Los Angeles, describes the underlying reason why recruits would subject themselves to such a rigorous training process: "They go on, practicing in obscurity, day after day, night after night, usually sleeping only four to six hours or at times even forgoing sleep altogether, hoping that the hard work and sacrifice will transform them from nameless trainees into megastars."[6]

H.O.T. Is the Future

Although the ethics of the Culture Technology training process has been called into question, Lee's K-pop star-making system was a huge success. In 1996 SME produced the first in a new generation of K-pop bands. One such group was H.O.T. (High-five of Teenagers), which had five members aged sixteen to eighteen. The concept of the band was based on a formula Lee developed after conducting polls in South Korean high schools. Female students were asked what they thought the ideal boy band would look and sound like. Lee listened, and he dressed H.O.T. in brightly colored, futuristic outfits. With their adorable faces and long shaggy hair, band members were groomed to induce screams of adoration from young girls.

H.O.T.'s music blended rap, EDM, slow romantic ballads, and a little rock and roll. The group's first album, *We Hate All Kinds of Violence*, was an instant success, selling eight hundred thousand copies in the first three months. The group's popularity was enhanced by the slightly rebellious ideas contained in its lyrics.

H.O.T. criticized South Korea's strict school system for stifling creativity and promoting bullying and violence. The 1997 video "We Are the Future" addressed these issues and was initially banned in South Korea. However, "We Are the Future" won an American MTV award for Best International Video.

Lee Soo-man (pictured) is considered the godfather of K-pop. Although the ethics of his training process has been called into question, Lee's star-making system has been a huge success.

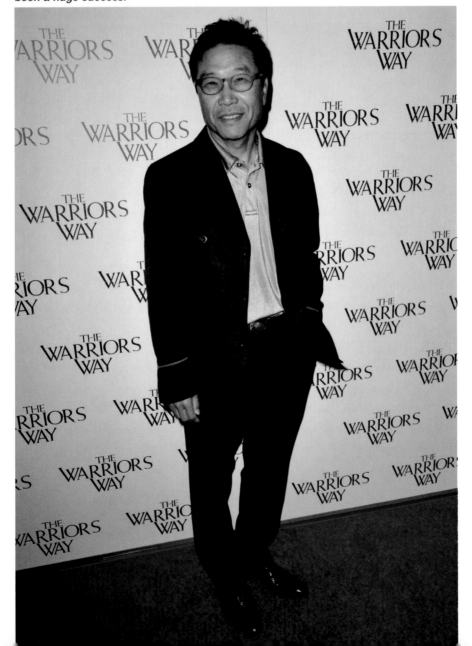

H.O.T. broke up in 2001 after a contract disagreement with SME. While H.O.T. sold millions of records, band members were only paid pennies for every album sold. (During this same time in the United States, record companies paid bands one to four dollars for every album sold.) During a four-year period of nearly nonstop work, each band member received $120,000, or around $30,000 annually, slightly more than the average wage of a South Korean schoolteacher.

K-Pop's Die-Hard Fans

South Koreans who love K-pop are considered the most dedicated and enthusiastic fans in the world. K-pop fangirls scream, jump, and faint when in the presence of their idols. Some even think of their favorite idols as boyfriends, husbands, and soul mates. Suk-Young Kim, professor of performance studies at the University of California, Los Angeles, describes the antics of fanatical fans:

> *Idols*, as the performers are often called, is a fitting term to capture the religious fervor the fans display in pursuing their heavily guarded favorites. Many support their stars via phone-in voting where charges apply, which allows them to debut or raise their rank on the music charts. Many purchase multiple copies of their stars' albums to increase sales revenue and gain access to promotional events where their idols make appearances. Some go on to become die-hard (*sasaeng*) fans, or the one who invade stars' lives to get their attention. Some will hire a [very fast] taxi to chase stars' vehicles; others will install hidden cameras to monitor stars' lives in private residences. Even more devious fans will go so far as to send toxic drinks to their stars or send love letters written in . . . blood, just to be remembered.

Suk-Young Kim, *K-Pop Live: Fans, Idols, and Multimedia Performance*. Stanford, CA: Stanford University Press, 2018, pp. 7–8.

Fanatical K-pop fans, known as *sasaeng* (diehards), blamed H.O.T.'s demise on Lee's business practices. Hundreds of teenage girls staged a protest at the offices of SME after the band announced its breakup. The protesters blocked roads, hurled eggs at the building, and tied up company phone lines with angry messages, including death threats.

Lee attempted to calm the situation by explaining that groups like H.O.T. received low royalty payments because they do not write and produce their own music. In addition, SME relied on successful artists like H.O.T. to help support seventy or so recruits in training at any given time. SME spent hundreds of thousands of dollars to develop each act, paying for costumes, instructors, chauffeurs, studio time, and language lessons, although most budding talents never achieve superstar status.

S.E.S. Breaks Records

H.O.T.'s breakup did little to slow Lee's dominance of K-pop. The company's first girl group, S.E.S., sold nearly as many records as H.O.T. had. S.E.S. was a trio that took its name from the initials of its band members, Sea, Eugene, and Shoo. Eugene was fifteen when she was hired from an audition tape. Shoo, also fifteen, was already in training at SME. Lee discovered the sixteen-year-old Sea singing at her high school.

S.E.S. released its self-titled first album, *S.E.S.*, in 1997. The album quickly sold 650,000 copies. In the video "I'm Your Girl," band members showed that S.E.S. was the female version of H.O.T., with hair, outfits, and dance moves that matched those of the boy band. When S.E.S. released the album *Love* in 1999, the record sold over 760,000 copies. This made *Love* the best-selling K-pop girl group album in history at that time.

By the early 2000s S.E.S. was presenting a more mature look and sound, performing jazz-flavored songs and rhythm and blues (R&B) ballads on its fourth album, *Letter from Greenland*. The new sound was not popular with fans, who were moving on to other groups. S.E.S broke up in 2003 as band members pursued solo singing and acting careers.

BoA's Best of Asia

While S.E.S. and H.O.T. sold millions of records, SME could not match the enormous sales generated by American teen idol bands like the Backstreet Boys, which sold nearly 100 million records from 1992 to 2000. K-pop producers were also having a difficult time competing with the Japanese version of the genre called J-pop. That changed in 2000 when the singer known as BoA appeared on the scene.

Kwon Boa, born in 1986, was only eleven years old when she auditioned for SME. Lee saw something special in the young girl's singing abilities and began developing her talents. She was given the name BoA, based on her last name. But fans have given her nicknames derived from the letters that include Best of Asia and Beat of an Angel. BoA spent two years in intense training, perfecting her singing and dancing talents. She was also taught to speak fluent Japanese and English.

BoA was only thirteen when her debut album *ID; Peace B* was released. Music on the album was strongly influenced by American hip-hop and popular R&B singers of the era, including Janet Jackson and Nelly. The upbeat, urban dance pop sound was an instant hit with K-pop fans. *ID; Peace B* sold 220,000 copies in South Korea and peaked at number ten on the pop charts. After BoA's initial success, her producers began marketing her aggressively in Japan.

BoA moved to Japan in 2002 and released her first Japanese album, *Listen to My Heart*, which sold over 1 million copies. This made BoA the first person to score a number one debut album in Japan in more than twenty years. The fact that she was South Korean made the achievement even more impressive. As her popularity continued to soar, BoA recorded with several high-profile artists, including Howie D of the Backstreet Boys and the Japanese hip-hop group m-flo.

Like many first-generation K-pop artists, BoA's popularity continued well into the twenty-first century. And BoA's fans seem to have changed little over the years. In 2010 Canadian K-pop journalists Simon Stawski and Martina Stawski described the near hysteria when BoA took the stage at the Asia Song Festival at the Seoul Olympic Stadium: "When BoA went on, we couldn't hear the show. Like, not at all. Why? Because the people . . . [were] screaming the whole time. And not regular screaming. It was cold outside, and one of the girls was screaming so much that her face was covered in sweat. No joke."[7]

> "When BoA went on, we couldn't hear the show. Like, not at all. Why? Because the people . . . [were] screaming the whole time."[7]
>
> —Simon Stawski and Martina Stawski, K-pop journalists

Super Junior: Kings of the Hallyu Wave

In the world of K-pop, BoA, H.O.T., and other top acts from the 1990s and early 2000s are considered the first generation of K-pop stars. However, by the mid-2000s new ways of buying and promoting K-pop music made the sound increasingly popular in China, Southeast Asia, the United States, and Europe. For example, the iTunes digital media store opened in 2003, Facebook was founded in 2004, and YouTube went live in 2005. South Korean producers were quick to take advantage of these game-changing digital outlets. For the first time, they began marketing K-pop music to listeners all over the world.

The boy band Super Junior was one of the first to benefit from the growing international interest in K-pop. The group was assembled by SME between 2000 and 2004 after auditions were held in Seoul, Los Angeles, and Beijing, China. At its peak, Super

Junior featured thirteen boys who were former models, actors, radio hosts, and MCs. While each had a specific talent such as singing, rapping, or dancing, band members were picked because they resembled the long-haired boys with large eyes and long eyelashes seen in Japanese comic books called shōjo manga. This style of manga, popular among teenage girls in Asia, is filled with romantic stories and family drama.

Super Junior, seen here performing in 2018, was one of the first bands to benefit from the growing international interest in K-pop. The group formed during the early 2000s.

Super Junior, also known as SJ and SuJu, debuted in 2005, and its first album, *Super Junior 05*, was an instant hit in South Korea and other parts of Asia. The group promoted itself to international audiences by offering the single "U" as a free download from its official website. "U" is driven by powerful harmonies, sharp electronic drum snaps, and a radio-friendly sound that would not be out of place on a 1980s album by pop star Michael Jackson. "U" generated over 400,000 downloads within five hours of its release and eventually exceeded 1.7 million downloads.

Super Junior was one of the first K-pop bands to take advantage of its growing popularity and form subgroups. Three Super Junior members, Kyuhyun, Ryeowook, and Yesung, performed in a band they called Super Junior-K.R.Y. Another subgroup, Super Junior-M, featured Han Geng, the only Chinese member of the band. The *M* stands for "Mandarin," the official language of China. As a result, Super Junior-M was extremely well received in China and went on to become the best-selling subgroup of Super Junior. Due to his success, in China Han was given the nickname King of Popularity.

In 2009 Super Junior got back together to record the album *Sorry, Sorry*. With its catchy electronically altered vocals, tight dance grooves, and seamless harmonies, *Sorry, Sorry* quickly hit number one and went on to win ten music awards. The album was the best-selling K-pop record in Thailand, China, Hong Kong, the Philippines, and Taiwan the year it was released. As Super Junior's fan base continued to grow, the group was nicknamed King of the Hallyu Wave.

Girls' Generation

Super Junior was so successful that SME formed the sister group Girls' Generation. The band's nine members were either winners of talent shows or recruits from modeling and acting agencies. The group's debut album, *Girls' Generation*, released in 2007, produced several hit singles, including "Baby Baby," "Kissing You," and the title track, "Girls' Generation." Three of the band's members, Jessica, Tiffany, and Sunny, were born in Southern California and were featured on several songs with English lyrics. According to Tiffany, Girls' Generation was striving to compete with Beyoncé, one of the biggest pop stars of the twenty-first century: "We definitely like to sing in English. We need to be nine Beyoncés."[8]

While Girls' Generation never got as big as Beyoncé in the United States, the group was extremely popular in South Korea. When the single "Gee" was released in 2009 the song reached number one on South Korean record charts within two days. After the video of "Gee" was posted on YouTube, it received 1 million views its first day. The video begins with nine band members posing as clothing store mannequins. After the store closes, they come to life and begin singing and dancing.

"We definitely like to sing in English. We need to be nine Beyoncés."[8]

—Tiffany, member of Girls' Generation

"Gee" was credited with changing popular South Korean clothing styles overnight. Fans who saw the video rushed out to buy the tight T-shirts and brightly colored pants showed off by the singers in Girls' Generation. And Seoul stores quickly ran short of supplies.

In a November 2011 interview, SME representative Kim Young Min stated that it cost about $2.5 million to train the nine members of Girls' Generation. But the investment paid off. Girls' Generation played sold-out concerts throughout Asia and even warmed up for the American alt-rock band Red Hot Chili Peppers when it toured in Japan. The group made its American TV debut on the *Late Show with David Letterman* in 2012, performing an English-language version of the hit single "The Boys."

Girls' Generation was so popular in South Korea that the group was nicknamed the Nation's Singers. By 2012 the group had sold more than 30 million singles and 4.4 million albums. Today songs like "Gee" and "I Got a Boy" are considered K-pop classics, while Girls' Generation is seen as a milestone K-pop group that helped popularize the sound in the United States.

While most people in the West were not aware of K-pop in the early 2000s, the tsunami of sound generated by Girls' Generation, H.O.T., Psy, and others reshaped modern musical history. Few can match the sights and sounds produced by highly trained K-pop performers singing and dancing together in synchronized precision. Flawless performances, irresistible beats, and international buzz laid the foundation for a K-pop wave that would soon engulf the world.

CHAPTER TWO

K-Pop Musicians of Influence

Korea has ancient musical traditions that date back thousands of years. But the first pop music was introduced to the country by American soldiers fighting in the Korean War during the early 1950s. Even though the war ended in 1953, many Americans remained stationed on more than two dozen military bases around the country. By the mid-1950s, soldiers were listening to the rock and roll sounds of Bill Haley & His Comets, Elvis Presley, Little Richard, and Chuck Berry. However, the music was considered immoral and was banned by South Korea's military government. Korean kids who wanted to rock had to find a way around the censorship. They surreptitiously bought records from American soldiers and played them in teahouses run by progressive owners.

Shin Joong-hyun was among the teenagers who listened to American rockers. Shin learned to play guitar and decided to become a rock star. In 1957 he changed his name to Jackie Shin and joined a band that entertained soldiers at music clubs and on American army bases. In 2011 Shin recalled his first gig: "The GIs were shouting, 'Hey shorty! Play [a] guitar solo!' . . . I played my first guitar solo . . . the crowd went wild, and the bandleader raised my wage by 50%."[9]

In 1962 Shin formed Add4, one of South Korea's first rock groups. Add4 released several singles driven by Shin's melodic guitar playing, which was influenced by Western groups like the Beatles and the Rolling Stones. However, Add4 had trouble finding an audience and eventually broke up. In 1967 Shin's music took on a new dimension when he heard the swirling psychedelic sounds of Jimi Hendrix, Iron Butterfly, and the Jefferson Airplane blasting from radios on American military bases. Shin performed Jefferson Airplane's "Somebody to Love" on a TV show and quickly became South Korea's most famous rock star. He started to write, produce, and perform his own music. Shin also composed and produced hits for other South Korean acts, including a female folksinger named Kim Jung-mi and a pop duo known as the Pearl Sisters.

> "I played my first guitar solo . . . the crowd went wild, and the bandleader raised my wage by 50%."[9]
>
> —Jackie Shin, South Korean rock musician

Today Shin is known as Korea's Godfather of Rock. However, during the late 1960s, government authorities considered Shin highly controversial. At the time, South Korea was run by a military regime headed by Park Chung-hee. Park built up South Korean automobile and electronics manufacturing industries, which transformed the impoverished nation into an economic powerhouse. But Park believed Shin's music was corrupting the nation's youth. Shin was at the height of his career in 1972 when Park banned his music from being played on the radio and ordered him to stop performing.

After Park died in 1979, the ban on Shin's music was lifted—but Korean tastes had changed. The late 1970s was an era that featured syrupy love ballads and bubblegum music, upbeat sounds with innocent lyrics written for mainstream tastes. Few Koreans were interested in hearing Shin's experimental rock.

Seo Taiji and Boys

By the 1980s disco music was popular in South Korea, and Shin found it very difficult to earn a living playing his music. To keep South Korean rock alive, Shin opened a Seoul nightclub called the Woodstock Bar in 1986. Shin's club, which featured local rock bands, provided an inspirational environment that influenced a young boy from Seoul named Seo Taiji. Seo started visiting the all-ages club as a teenager and went on to become the first K-pop star.

During the Korean War, American soldiers stationed in Korea were listening to rock and roll acts like Elvis Presley. The music was considered immoral and was banned by South Korea's government, but that didn't stop Korean kids from listing to the music.

In 1987, when he was seventeen, Seo was asked to play bass in the heavy metal group Sinawe, which was performing at the Woodstock Bar. Music quickly took precedence over schoolwork, and Seo dropped out of high school to play in Sinawe. This was an extremely rebellious act in Korean culture, which places a very high value on education. Sinawe had several fairly successful albums but broke up in 1991.

By that time, however, Seo was finding new inspiration in the rhythmic poetry of rap. He decided to create an entirely new sound by melding hip-hop with pop and a defiant punk rock attitude. Seo experimented with what was then a new technology called musical instrument digital interface (MIDI). MIDI combines electronic musical instruments like keyboard synthesizers and drum machines with computer software. The resulting technology allows users to play, record, and edit music.

In addition to creating a new sound, Seo wanted to include attention-getting dance moves in his performances. To this end, he hired a skilled dancer named Yang Hyun-suk to give him lessons. Yang thought Seo's music was amazing and proposed they start a group. After joining forces Seo and Yang hired one of South Korea's top dancers, Lee Juno, to form a trio called Seo Taiji and Boys.

In 1992 Seo Taiji and Boys made its first public appearance on a South Korean TV talent show, on which they performed a rowdy song called "Nan Arayo" ("I Know"). The song was propelled by a fresh sound called new jack swing, which had first been pioneered by pop singer Janet Jackson. New jack swing blends several musical elements, including rap lyrics, catchy choruses, hip-hop beats, dance pop synthesizers, and bass-heavy R&B growls.

The group's moves were as unique as the music. Seo Taiji and Boys performed a dance called formation changing. This style features exaggerated moves such as wild jumping, kicking, and thrusting one's arms in the air. The show's judges—and members of the studio audience—were shocked. Seo Taiji and Boys received the lowest possible rating from the talent jury.

The adults might have been bewildered by the performance, but "Nan Arayo" was a hit with the kids watching at home. The song reached number one on the South Korean music charts and stayed there for a record-breaking seventeen weeks. K-pop historian Hannah Waitt explains the group's impact: "Seo Taiji and the Boys created a completely new genre that distinguished the music of the youth from the music of the adults. For the first time, someone was writing music that kids and teenagers could relate to. . . . Because of this, to this day most industry professionals name the exact date of Seo Taiji and the Boys' debut performance as the definitive beginning of K-pop."[10]

In 1992 Seo Taiji and Boys released its eponymous debut album, *Seo Taiji and Boys*, which further enhanced the band's reputation among its fans. The lyrics were critical of society and the South Korean school system, which Seo blamed for brainwashing children. Few Korean entertainers had ever touched on these sensitive topics. This helped popularize the band in Japan, which had an equally strict school system.

The President of Culture

Most musicians who are lucky enough to have a hit album attempt to reproduce the sounds that brought them their initial success. Seo broke this rule, however. He refused to stick with the hip-hop dance formula, drawing instead from his heavy metal background to produce several hard-edged songs for the group's third album, *Seo Taiji and Boys III* (1994). The song "Classroom Idea" borders on hard-core industrial metal, a style characterized by shrieking vocals, pounding drums, and muddy, distorted guitar sounds.

K-Pop's Big Three Production Companies

Almost every influential K-pop act since the 1990s owes its success to one of South Korea's Big Three production companies: SM Entertainment, YG Entertainment, and JYP Entertainment.

Lee Soo-man kicked off the K-pop revolution when he founded SM Entertainment in 1989. This company focuses on producing colorful K-pop music acts such as BoA and Super Junior, who do not write their own songs and are as famous for their looks as their music.

YG Entertainment was created in 1996 by Yang Hyun-suk, a former member of Seo Taiji and Boys. YG is known for producing R&B and hip-hop groups, including top artists like Psy and the girl group 2NE1. The company emphasizes its commitment to artistic freedom, and most YG acts write and produce their own music.

JYP Entertainment was founded in 1997 by Park Jin-Young. Park had a successful career as a K-pop solo artist in the early 1990s but felt he was too old to maintain his status as a teen idol. Park is a hands-on producer who oversees development of all his company's acts. Park created K-pop stars, including the Wonder Girls, g.o.d., and 2PM. He invested half a million dollars developing Rain into an international K-pop sensation. And while Rain's talents might have been impressive, Park criticized him constantly. As Rain recalls, "I thought if could satisfy Park Jin-young, I would be able to satisfy anyone in the world."

Quoted in Mark James Russell, *Pop Goes Korea*. Berkeley, CA: Stone Bridge, 2008, pp. 147–48.

Seo's rebellious attitude carried over to the South Korean music industry. During this era young music fans were aggressively targeted by record companies that ran seemingly endless media promotions for pop groups. Seo believed this crass type of music promotion diminished his art. Rather than make public appearances as requested by his record label, Seo became a recluse who rarely appeared in public. Ironically, this only added to the singer's mystique and further boosted his popularity.

Seo Taiji performs in 2008. He became the first K-pop star when he formed the group Seo Taiji and Boys in the early 1990s.

By 1996 Seo felt his music was suffering due to the band's rigorous recording and performing schedule. In an unprecedented move for a Korean pop band, Seo Taiji and Boys broke up at the height of their popularity. Although the group disappeared, its four studio albums and three live albums continued to resonate. As Korean studies professor Roald Maliangkay explains,

[Seo's] band had an enormous influence on young people's ideas on music, dance and fashion, and even on the Korean language and forms of communication. When in August 1997 a survey was carried out to find out what

30

Koreans considered their most important cultural product, the band came out on top, ranked even higher than the Korean alphabet.[11]

After Seo Taiji and Boys broke up, Yang Hyun-suk founded YG Entertainment, which grew into one of South Korea's "Big Three" K-pop production powerhouses, along with SM Entertainment and JYP Entertainment. Seo went on to launch a successful solo career in 1998 and continued to produce groundbreaking music. His 2000 album, *Ultramania*, melds a number of styles, including alternative rock, hard-core punk, and heavy metal.

In 2012 Seo celebrated his twentieth anniversary in the music business. By this time his fans had given him the nickname the President of Culture. As a free-thinking innovator, Seo laid the foundation for modern K-pop while pushing the musical boundaries of South Korean music in ways that were felt for decades. Of Korean pop, music producer Koh Young-whan says, "There were two eras. Before Seo Taiji and after Seo Taiji."[12]

Dancing like a Rainy Day

The first era of Korean pop music was mainly enjoyed by fans in South Korea and Japan. But during the music's second wave, an idol known as Rain became an international star who was responsible for introducing K-pop sounds to the West.

Rain was born Jung Ji-hoon in 1982 in a poor Seoul neighborhood. He developed a passion for dancing at age six while watching the unique dance moves of Michael Jackson on MTV Korea. In sixth grade Jung won a talent contest for his impressive imitation of Jackson. By the time he was in high school, Jung was hanging out on Seoul street corners with other pop-obsessed teenagers who performed dance routines for one another while dreaming of stardom.

At age eighteen Jung attempted to embark on a solo career. He practiced relentlessly and auditioned constantly but was rejected by eighteen music management companies. According to K-pop writer Mark James Russell, Jung did not fit the typical mold of a K-pop idol: "No one was interested in the tall, slightly awkward-looking teenager. At the time, the main look for male singers in Korea was cute, like the young boys who looked like they stepped out of the pages of a . . . manga."[13]

Jung's luck changed in 2000 after a passing a four-hour audition for K-pop producer Park Jin-Young, founder of JYP Entertainment. After Jung was recruited, he performed monthly at JYP contests held for recruits. Jung won twelve of the monthly showcases in a row, setting a record. Park eventually decided Jung was ready for the big time. He gave the unknown singer the name Bi, Korean for "rain." In 2006 Park explained his choice: "There was something sad about him then, and there still is, something cool and gloomy."[14] Jung was happy with the new name, saying, "When I'm dancing I give off the feeling of a rainy day."[15]

Rain's 2002 introductory album, *Bad Guy*, was not an overwhelming success by K-pop standards. But his second album, *Ways to Avoid the Sun* (2003), made him a K-pop idol. In 2004 Rain bolstered his popularity by starring in a popular televised K-drama, *Full House*. The show made Rain an international celebrity when it aired in more than a dozen nations, including the Philippines, Indonesia, Thailand, China, Japan, Turkey, Morocco, and Israel. The show also ran in the United States on ImageAsian TV with English subtitles. Rain's third album, *It's Raining* (2004), was a mammoth success, selling over 1 million copies and topping the charts in Korea, Japan, Indonesia, and Thailand. The album features Rain's smooth crooning and rapping over a synth-heavy EDM sound. The next year, Rain was the biggest star in South Korea.

2NE1

In 2009 the girl group 2NE1 gained instant recognition in South Korea when it became the first K-pop band to debut in a television commercial. After the video of "Lollipop" was used in a cell phone ad by electronics giant LG, the song went on to sell over 3.3 million digital downloads. Following the success of "Lollipop," nearly every Korean TV ad had its own song featuring a K-pop band.

YG Entertainment, which created the band, says *2NE1* stands for "new evolution of the twenty-first century." But fans have nicknamed the band To Anyone. Whatever the band was called, its four members—Bom, CL, Dara, and Minzy—were very influential on the next generation of K-pop girl groups.

2NE1 followed the success of "Lollipop" with an EP and a full-length album that featured a chart-topping futuristic synth-pop sound. Group members also released solo albums. By 2011 2NE1 was attracting widespread international attention for its unique style. Band members cultivated a tough, edgy image. They rejected the traditional brightly colored girl-group styles in favor of black leather goth punk outfits. During the band's heyday from 2009 to 2014, 2NE1 toured the United States, worked with American rapper and producer will.i.am of the Black Eyed Peas, and set K-pop chart records in the United States and South Korea. The group went on hiatus in 2015, with band members pursuing solo careers; 2NE1 officially disbanded in 2017.

As a result, Rain was *everywhere*. His image was used to endorse a variety of products in magazines, in TV commercials, and on billboards. MTV Asia gave Rain numerous video and music awards and named him Star of the Year.

Rain's 2006 international tour, Rain's Coming, featured an extravagant stage show designed by a production company that had previously worked with Michael Jackson, Madonna, Britney Spears, and the Rolling Stones. Rain visited numerous cities in Asia and the United States, and his tour grossed more than $100 million. When the Rain's Coming tour visited Madison Square Garden in New York City, tickets sold out in a matter of days.

The *New York Times* labeled Rain as the South Korean Justin Timberlake and described his fanatical fans as possessed with "Rain-mania."[16] *Time* magazine also took note in 2006, listing Rain in the article "100 Most Influential People Who Shape Our World." That year Rain also made *People*'s list of the Most Beauti-

Superstar Rain performs in 2011. The New York Times *called Rain the South Korean Justin Timberlake and described his fanatical fans as possessed with "Rain-mania."*

ful People in the world. He also branched out into movies. His role in the 2009 *Ninja Assassin* earned him the Biggest Badass Award at the 2010 MTV Movie Awards.

Despite the accolades, Rain has not let success go to his head. He continues to work diligently on his career, making new music and performing at concerts throughout the world. Park attributes Rain's work ethic to a sense of obligation to his late mother: "He promised his mom that he was going to be the No. 1 singer in the whole world. That's why he never parties, never drinks, never goes out and practices hours every day."[17]

Psy's Psycho World

Rain owed his success to his years of training at a K-pop production studio. Rapper Psy, on the other hand, rose to the top despite the powerful K-pop industry. He also struggled for more than a decade before "Gangnam Style" made him an international superstar. But like Seo and some other K-pop notables, Psy rebelled against his parents, ignored his studies, and took inspiration from Western music videos on South Korean television.

Psy was born Park Jae-sang in Seoul in 1977. When he was fifteen, he became obsessed with the British rock band Queen. Psy especially loved Queen's 1975 live performance of "Bohemian Rhapsody" at Wembley Stadium in London. The video ignited an interest in music and motivated Psy to attend the respected Berklee College of Music in Boston. However, as Psy told *Rolling Stone* magazine in 2012, he was not all that interested in schoolwork: "I was a freshman for four years. Class was too early, so I didn't go. . . . I bought some computers and media stuff with the tuition and started making beats."[18]

When Psy was not creating hip-hop beats with electronic keyboards and audio recording software, he was studying English so he could better understand the gangsta rappers he saw on MTV. Psy was captivated by the era's most popular rappers, such as

Tupac Shakur, Snoop Dogg, and Eminem. With the influence of their music, Psy developed his own brand of Korean rap music and dropped out of college in 1999. He returned to Seoul in 2000 to pitch his music to the Big Three K-pop companies. Label executives appreciated Psy's music, but there was a problem—they did not like the way he looked. "They suggested plastic surgery right in front of me," he remembers, adding that the executives would say things like, "'We gotta change something, for example, your face?'"[19]

Psy understood that he did not look like Rain or other K-pop idols. But instead of surgically altering his face, he decided to record and release his own music. This was an unusual move in the South Korean music industry, which has always been tightly controlled by a few companies. But it gave Psy a musical advantage—he did not have to conform to typical K-pop standards, which dictated how artists sang, danced, looked, and even spoke. Psy went wherever his artistic inspirations took him.

Psy released a series of albums that were controversial from the start. His debut album, *PSY from the Psycho World!* (2001), included the rap song "I Love Sex." The song prompted South Korean government censors to investigate Psy and fine him for what they regarded as inappropriate lyrics. The media piled on too. When Psy performed his jerky dance moves on TV, he was mockingly nicknamed the Bizarre Singer.

Psy's behavior offstage also attracted government attention. In late 2001 he was arrested and fined for smoking marijuana. Rather than tone down his sound or image, Psy wrote songs about the controversies; these were featured on his second album, *Sa 2*, or *Adults Only*. Numerous Korean civil groups, including the Ministry of Gender Equality and Family, complained about the record. Sales of it were restricted to adults over age nineteen.

Reviewers loved Psy, but the uproar over his lyrics and the restrictions on his album sales nearly ended his career. By 2010 he was out of money and ready to leave the music business. However, his albums had attracted so much attention that YG Entertainment was motivated to offer him a recording contract. The record deal gave Psy a second chance. His next album, *PSYFive*, received several Asian music awards.

But Psy's big break came in January 2012 when he played a live showcase in Osaka, Japan, with popular K-pop bands BigBang and 2NE1. The show, called the YG Family Concert, was attended by eighty thousand K-pop fans and broadcast on Japanese national TV. Psy used his self-effacing sense of humor to his advantage. He walked onstage and held up a sign, written in Japanese: "I'm a famous singer well-known for driving the audience wild in Korea, but here, today, I'm just a little chubby newcomer."[20] He then began rapping and performing outrageous dance moves that imitated Lady Gaga and Beyoncé. The audience went wild.

The Osaka performance made Psy realize that humor and goofy dancing might be the key to his success. He began working on the silliest dance moves he could imagine. He considered panda and kangaroo dances but ultimately settled on moves that mimicked a rider trotting on an invisible horse. He put his dance moves to work when making a video for "Gangnam Style," a song from his sixth album, *PSY 6 (Six Rules), Part 1*. "Gangnam Style" proved to by Psy's game changer. Within a month the video shot to number one on YouTube's Most Viewed Video chart, a first for any South Korean artist. By this time Psy was thirty-five years old, ancient by K-pop standards.

With "Gangnam Style" Psy achieved the international success that had long eluded him. He was soon seen trotting out "Gangnam Style" on television sets from Australia to South America. And in October 2012 Psy received perhaps the most unusual honor of all. Despite his continual battle over obscene lyrics, Psy was recognized by the United Nations as an "international sensation" and met with United Nations chief and South Korean native Ban Ki-moon. Ban told reporters that

Psy's music had great powers that attracted international audiences and helped people overcome intolerance. At the end of 2012, Psy was named one of *Rolling Stone* magazine's Game Changers of the Year. He signed a management contract with Justin Bieber's manager, Scooter Braun.

Psy achieved fame by breaking away from rigid cultural expectations and a tightly controlled music industry. Through it all, Psy remained humble, telling *Rolling Stone*, "I was not the best, but I did my best. All the time."[21] By putting his own spin on hip-hop and adding an element of humor, Psy will always be remembered, along with Jackie Shin and Seo Taiji, as an innovator who reinvented the sounds of Korean pop music for a new generation.

CHAPTER THREE

Creating a Following

K-pop artists are famous for combining multiple musical elements in their songs, including rap, rock, pop, R&B, and EDM. Then, they top off their musical confections with over-the-top dances and outrageous fashion. But this brilliant blend of entertainment would be largely unknown outside South Korea were it not for the skillful use of social media by K-pop idols. These stars, and their record companies, are experts at promoting their music to global audiences through YouTube, celebrity Twitter and Instagram accounts, Facebook postings, live streaming, and vlogs (video blogs).

K-pop acts rely on hashtags, retweets, and viral videos to expand their reach in regions where their music is ignored by radio programmers. And in a phenomenon unique to K-pop, fans of some groups volunteer their own time and resources to promote their favorite idols online and in other media. This feedback loop of bands and social media fandom has helped some K-pop bands push their music sales to record heights, as has fantastically flashy videos that capture the imagination.

Creating Eye- and Ear-Catching Videos

Ever since Psy's "Gangnam Style" video brought K-pop to the masses in 2012, YouTube has been ground zero for K-pop bands hoping to gain worldwide attention. With this in mind, K-pop music video producers strive to provide a treat for both the eyes and ears by including vividly colored costumes, spectacular dance routines, and complex story lines. K-pop bands understand that if they focus on these key visual elements, people will be more likely to share their videos. K-pop videos also include a few English phrases meant to attract clicks and likes from Western viewers.

One of the biggest K-pop bands, BlackPink, exemplifies how to create a following and keep fans engaged through the use of specific songwriting and video-production techniques. BlackPink's 2018 music video, "Ddu-Du Ddu-Du," is a perfect example of how dress, dance, plot, and English lyrics combine to create a viral sensation. "Ddu-Du Ddu-Du" racked up nearly 740 million YouTube views and helped BlackPink become the first K-pop group to attract more than 20 million YouTube subscribers. As the group said in a statement, "[YouTube has] helped us reach out and share our music [with] millions of people around the world."[22]

When "Ddu-Du Ddu-Du" begins, the four band members—Rosé, Jennie, Lisa, and Jisoo—chant "BlackPink" in English. The video uses a hot pink color scheme throughout the video, juxtaposed with black to reinforce the band's name. The video even features a pink and red cockatoo. Brilliant colors highlight the performers' outfits, lipstick, and hair coloring. In various scenes bursts of pink smoke, yellow flames, and purple and blue backdrops blend into a beautiful artistic potpourri.

K-pop producers understand that a good plot is important to any story. And the plotline of "Ddu-Du Ddu-Du" can be understood even by those who do not speak Korean. "Ddu-Du Ddu-Du" portrays the band members as independent, slightly dangerous women who are in charge when it comes to their relationships with men. The scenes are carefully crafted to portray band members as strong, sassy, and confident. The messages are reinforced by Lisa wielding a samurai sword, Jennie riding a glamourous mirrored tank, and Jisoo pushing past dozens of men trying to photograph her.

The choreographed dance routines also help tell the story without using words. Band members look directly into the camera and shake and point their fingers like weapons at viewers. The tough message is reinforced when the girls yell out an expression in English that includes the song's title. Media reviewer Rowena

Female K-pop band BlackPink, seen performing in 2017, created a following through YouTube. The band became the first K-pop group to attract more than 20 million YouTube subscribers.

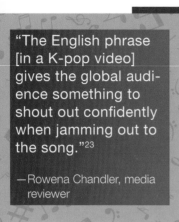

Chandler explains how K-pop bands use this linguistic trick: "The English phrase gives the global audience something to shout out confidently when jamming out to the song, and also is an indicator of what the song happens to be about."[23]

While the dance routines are complicated, fans at home can still work out some of the steps and share them with their friends. According to Chandler, "Dancing makes [K-pop videos] engaging and entertaining to watch, as well as providing a common form of communication for the viewers to follow along with and start doing themselves. It's a connector between artist and fan."[24] Like many recently released K-pop videos, "Ddu-Du Ddu-Du" also includes English subtitles. This makes it easier for millions of fans in the United States and elsewhere to understand the lyrics and connect with the music.

BTS Writes Its Own Songs

For fans of BTS, the boy band's lyrics are as important as its dance routines and wild costumes. As BTS fan Daphne Kwong explains, "The members of BTS write their own songs and their lyrics resonate with fans."[25]

The fact that the seven band members—V, J-Hope, RM, Jin, Jimin, Jungkook, and Suga—compose and produce much of their music sets them apart. Most K-pop idols sing songs written by teams of highly paid professionals;

SM Entertainment (SME) holds two songwriting conferences annually in South Korea, inviting about three hundred composers from around the world to participate. The lyrics turned out by these professionals rarely mention political or social issues.

But BTS does not shy away from controversial statements, as Suga notes: "It isn't a BTS album if there isn't a track criticizing society."[26]

For example, the lyrics to BTS's first single, "No More Dream" (2013), take aim at overbearing parents who stop their children from pursuing their dreams. Other BTS songs address

BlackPink

BlackPink is a megastar girl group that has consistently topped the K-pop charts since the release of its first hit beat-heavy single, "Boombayah," in 2016. The "Boombayah" video quickly attracted over 100 million views on YouTube, setting a record for K-pop bands. Since that time BlackPink has become an international sensation, with its infectious blend of hip-hop, EDM, and rock. When the group announced it was playing Tokyo's Budokan arena in 2017, over two hundred thousand people attempted to purchase tickets for the fourteen-thousand-seat venue. But it was the single "Ddu-Du Ddu-Du" that pushed BlackPink into the superstar stratosphere. Within a week of its 2018 release, the song was streamed over 12.5 million times in the United States while peaking at number one on record charts in numerous countries.

BlackPink was at the height of its popularity in 2019 when it made history as the first female K-pop band to play at the Coachella Valley Music and Arts Festival in Indio, California. After seeing the performance, reviewer Rhian Daly explained why BlackPink has become an unstoppable musical force:

> There are huge screams from the audience for every pop or strut of dynamic choreography, every time rappers Jennie and Lisa growl their lines with that bit more intensity than on record, every time singers Rosé and Jisoo nail their soaring melodies. The women on stage are clearly enjoying it as much as the people they're performing for, too—their faces are an almost permanent display for broad, genuine grins.

Rhian Daly, "In a Big Week for K-Pop Stateside, BLACKPINK's History-Making Coachella Debut Is as Impressive as They Come," NME, April 13, 2019. www.nme.com.

racism, South Korea's culture of materialism, and clinical depression. Even the band's name is unusual for a K-pop act. In Korean *BTS* stands for "Bangtan Sonyeondan," which translates to "Bulletproof Boy Scouts." Rapper and lead dancer J-Hope explains the meaning of the name: "It means to block out stereotypes, criticisms, and expectations that [take] aim on adolescents like bullets, to preserve the values and ideal of today's adolescents."[27]

BTS Makes a Name for Itself on Social Media

BTS preserved its values by ignoring the Big Three production companies and signing with a small start-up called Big Hit Entertainment in 2010. Unlike the Big Three, Big Hit could not promote the band using expensive media campaigns and appearances on South Korean television shows. BTS solved this problem by creatively using social media to make a name for itself. The band opened a Twitter account in 2011, started a YouTube channel in 2012, and began releasing audio tracks on the SoundCloud streaming service. Coincidentally, during these years social media use among the general public began to expand rapidly as well. As journalist Aja Romano explains, by utilizing social media channels expertly, "BTS would go on to completely transform the image of all-male boy bands in South Korean music and shatter conceptions of what breakout success looked like for South Korean bands overseas."[28]

In 2013 BTS again relied on social media to promote its debut album, *2 Cool 4 Skool*. The group placed a clock on its website to count down to the exact moment the album would be released. A forty-six-second video about the album, called a teaser trailer, was uploaded to YouTube. Photos of the seven band members were posted on the group's official Facebook page, and the album's track list was revealed on Twitter. Two days before the album's release, a music video for "No More Dreams" appeared on K-pop fan websites and YouTube. The

K-pop band BTS, accepting a music award in 2017, has experimented with new social media applications. It was the first group to broadcast a concert on the live-streaming mobile app V Live.

song entered the *Billboard* World Digital Songs charts by the end of June and stayed there for three weeks. The album *2 Cool 4 Skool* also peaked at number five on South Korea's Gaon Album Chart. With very little investment in promotion, BTS had its first commercial success.

By 2014 BTS was performing concerts in South Korea and Japan and selling hundreds of thousands of albums. The group also made its debut in the United States, appearing as the top-billed act at the Los Angeles K-pop convention, KCON.

Making Intimate Connections with Fans

While BTS was attracting new fans, band members remained prolific users of social media. They personally recorded video diaries, posted dance practices, took part in postconcert chats, and answered fan questions on Twitter. These online interactions helped fans feel a close connection to band members that they might not have had otherwise. And the connections helped create a demand for albums, merchandise, and concert tickets. As professor of Eastern studies Michelle Cho explains, "BTS's social media presence is the key to their popularity in North America and beyond, as well as the reason [why] they can sell out stadium shows from Sydney [Australia] to Osaka [Japan] to Santiago [Chile]."[29]

The key to BTS's success can be traced to its informal approach when compared to other K-pop artists. For example, the Twitter account for Girls' Generation is run by an SME company executive who posts advertisements for fan meeting events, TV appearances, and song releases. Each mem-

Breaking Records BTS Style

BTS skyrocketed to the top of the music charts through the skillful use of social media, which attracted an international audience. Driven by fan groups like the A.R.M.Y. and other dedicated BTS followers, the K-pop band has shattered one music industry record after another.

In May 2018 BTS became the first South Korean band in history to debut an album at number one on the *Billboard* 200 album chart with *Love Yourself: Tear*. This was also the first foreign-language number one album since 2006. At the same time the single "Fake Love" launched at number ten on *Billboard*'s Hot 100 chart, marking the first Hot 100 top ten ever for a K-pop group. The video for "Fake Love" was the first video by a K-pop band to reach 100 million views in under nine days. This broke the previous record held by BTS, whose 2018 video of "DNA" attracted 100 million views in twenty-four days.

The group broke its own record-setting album release a few months later with *Love Yourself: Answer*, which also hit number one. This album featured a collaboration with Nicki Minaj on a new version of the song "Idol." The music video for "Idol" hit 45 million views in its first twenty-four hours on YouTube. This broke a previous record held by pop star Taylor Swift.

ber of Girls' Generation has her own personal account, overseen by social media managers who sometimes write posts and coordinate various uploads. But the collective BTS Twitter account has been personal from the very beginning; only the seven band members contribute to it. This allows fans to engage individually with the performers and one another. As media analyst Jade Hookham writes, "Because BTS uses this shared-account format, fans have a single place where they can find entertaining content about their favorite group. . . . The BTS Twitter account is full of surprises. And although the majority of the Tweets are in Korean, the fans still eat it up."[30]

"BTS's social media presence is the key to their popularity in North America and beyond."[29]

—Michelle Cho, professor of Eastern studies

Broadcasting Live Performances

BTS has also been willing to experiment with new social media applications. In 2015 it was the first group to broadcast a concert on V Live, when the South Korean live-streaming mobile app by Naver was first introduced. BTS went on to use V Live to broadcast exclusive performances, promotional events, and showcases. The band also created a V Live series called *Run BTS!* The series, which had over seventy episodes by 2019, showed the band hanging out backstage, having tea, or even playing Pictionary.

V Live is popular throughout Asia, North America, and Europe. Whenever a broadcast goes live, an automatic push alarm is sent to users throughout the world. BTS live streams are instantly translated into English, and after a broadcast ends, subtitles in nine languages are added to archived episodes. V Live users can respond in real time, sharing their thoughts and adding heart symbols to their favorite clips.

By contradicting the norms of K-pop success, BTS grew into a record-breaking social media behemoth. According to data released by Twitter, members of BTS were the most tweeted-about celebrities in the world in 2017. The group recorded an average 252,231 retweets per tweet, four times more than its closest competitor, K-pop boy band Exo. These figures prove that the skillful use of social media helped BTS build an audience of fiercely loyal fans. As journalist E. Alex Jung writes, "BTS has been active on social media from the jump. . . . This gave the sense, particularly if you followed them early on, that you were in the trenches with them."[31]

Deploying the A.R.M.Y.

Cultivating die-hard fan groups are another way that K-pop acts generate and keep a following, and nearly every popular K-pop act has its own, dedicated groups. But the personalized posting by the boys in BTS helped create one of the most dedicated fan groups in the world of K-pop: the A.R.M.Y.

A.R.M.Y. is an abbreviation for "Adorable Representative M.C. for Youth." It is made up of hundreds of thousands of BTS fans, many of whom are in the United States. The American version of the BTS A.R.M.Y. is described by Jung as "of every demographic, but mostly young women—Asian, black, Latina, Arab, Native American, white, and every ethnic category those words could possibly [cover]."[32]

A.R.M.Y. members act as social media ambassadors for BTS. They make video compilations of individual band idols, editing together numerous clips of their favorite performers into a single short movie. And when BTS appears on Korean TV music shows, multilingual fans translate what the band is saying so non-Korean speakers can understand. A.R.M.Y. members also spend countless hours analyzing lyrics, discussing song themes, and picking apart supposedly hidden messages in photos and videos. For example, when the album *Love Yourself: Tear* was released in 2018, one A.R.M.Y. fan tweeted about her emotional reaction to the song "Fake Love": "It's almost 3hrs and I can't stop crying. The theory behind FAKE LOVE is haunting me. FAKE LOVE is when you love something/someone truly & madly & when you realize that everything was fake it hurts you forever."[33]

Burning Up Twitter for BTS

In 2017 members of the BTS A.R.M.Y. skillfully used Twitter to help their favorite band win the Top Social Artist Award at the Billboard Music Awards. This fan-voted category recognizes social media impact as measured in Twitter retweets and hashtags. When *Billboard* nominated BTS as the first-ever South Korean group to qualify for the award, the group was running against popular American artists such as Selena Gomez and Shawn Mendes. Justin Bieber had won the award every year since

Anxious fans wait in line for a BTS concert in Amsterdam. BTS has one of the most dedicated fan groups in the world of K-pop. The group is known as the A.R.M.Y. (Adorable Representative M.C. for Youth).

2011. But A.R.M.Y.s went to work as soon as polls opened, and the fan base delivered an astounding 300 million votes, according to the K-pop entertainment website Soompi. After winning, BTS performed to a large American television audience at the Billboard Music Awards. In an interview, BTS member RM acknowledged the impact his fan group had had on the win: "We won the Top Social Artist Award thanks to the dedication from our ARMYs around the world. Our honor and gratitude goes directly to them."[34]

A.R.M.Y.s operate several dedicated Twitter accounts specifically created to push the boy band to the top of the charts. The account BTS on Billboard! had nearly 850,000 followers as of 2019, and its home page says it is devoted to helping BTS "spread their wings & fly on the Billboard Charts."[35] BTS on Billboard! has seven administrators, each in a different time zone. When BTS releases new music, the administrators encourage fans to stream and buy the music. One of the administrators for BTS on Billboard!, known as CJ, explains that the account "made many people curious about BTS, which in turn made them want to look them up; it also opened several new doors for the group in the west."[36]

In 2018 there were at least two other specialized BTS Twitter accounts: BTS Views was dedicated to tracking the band's YouTube views, while BTS Voting Team is used to drive fans to hashtag-driven voting awards like the Billboard Music Awards. That same year, A.R.M.Y.s used Twitter to do something unheard of in the world of pop music. Fans organized a fund-raiser to buy ad space on billboards to promote BTS. A.R.M.Y.s raised around $30,000 to sponsor a BTS billboard for one week in Times Square, New York City's major commercial district and a tourist destination. Another legion made up of forty-six A.R.M.Y.s in Nashville, Tennessee, pulled together around $2,500 to purchase ad space on the electronic billboard known as the Nashville Sign, which greets visitors to the city. The Nashville BTS ad flashed 164 times a day for three weeks.

Jung explains how the use of Twitter and other social media outlets unites BTS and its A.R.M.Y. of fans:

> What's good for BTS is good for the Army, and rooting for them feels like rooting for yourself. Indeed, BigHit often makes sure to send out news updates through social channels . . . as well as official press releases, not just because it's an effective publicity mechanism, but because preserving a direct line of communication to the Army is crucial to the BTS experience.[37]

A Cinderella Story

When BTS plays concerts—like the sold-out show at the Citi Field baseball stadium in New York City in 2018—the loudest screams come when band members mention the A.R.M.Y. from the stage. BTS is very aware that A.R.M.Y.s are driving its success through the deft use of social media. As Jung notes, "Online, [the A.R.M.Y.'s] power is fearsome and vigilant. The boundaryless world-building of the internet has allowed the Army to flourish without regard for nation-states or cultural reproach, driving clicks, votes, and purchases."[38]

Band members pay back the A.R.M.Y.'s loyalty, and create personal connections, by providing a near-constant stream of tweets, posts, and uploads. While this personal connection occurs online only, the back-and-forth energy loop between A.R.M.Y.s and the band blurs the line between superstars and super fans. The band makes it seem like if BTS can make it big, anyone with a dream can follow in BTS's footsteps. As Jung puts it, "There isn't a better Cinderella story in K-pop than BTS, because if these seven kids from various corners of the Korean peninsula can make it against all odds, then why not you?"[39]

K-Pop's Reigning Royalty

The K-pop global music craze is bigger than ever, and BTS is its driving force. The seven members of BTS are selling more records and concert tickets globally than any other K-pop act—and even more than some Western pop acts. But the K-pop scene is competitive, and there are numerous other chart-topping groups attracting legions of dedicated fans. Acts like Exo have actually been singing, rapping, and dancing longer than BTS has. Others are newer to the scene and trying to stand out in what is becoming an increasingly crowded field. Some are even as popular as BTS in South Korea and elsewhere in Asia but are less well known on the international stage. The success of all of these groups is setting off what Korean studies professor Susanna Lim has called "an Asian invasion"[40] in the West.

Exo: Kings of K-Pop

If any K-pop group can come close to matching BTS in terms of YouTube views, Twitter followers, music downloads, and concert tickets sold, it would be another boy band with a three-letter name, Exo (stylized as EXO). The band has consistently ranked among the top five most influential performers on the *Forbes* Korea Power Celebrity list. South Koreans commonly refer to Exo as the biggest boy band in the world and have nicknamed the group the Kings of K-pop.

Unlike BTS, which retained all seven original members, Exo has had a revolving cast of idols. Even devotees of the band might be confused about the makeup of the group. Exo was created in 2012 by SME founder Lee Soo-man, who sought to take advantage of the growing interest in K-pop music in China and Japan. He auditioned singers and dancers from South Korea and China for two independent subgroups: Exo-K and Exo-M. The subgroups performed the same melodic dance pop hits, influenced by hip-hop, R&B, and EDM. The six boys in Exo-K sang in Korean and played in South Korea and Japan. The guys in Exo-M, however, most of whom were from China, recorded in Mandarin and focused their music and live performances on the Chinese market.

Although the two Exo subgroups played the same music, the bands had different defining characteristics. Exo-K exuded a youthful and innocent image, while Exo-M was more mature and slightly dangerous. This led fans to believe that the *K* stood for "kids" while *M* stood for "men." In 2014 the two subgroups combined into a single group but continued to release and perform music in multiple languages. However, three members quit the group at this time, leaving Exo with nine performers. And in 2016 three band members formed another subgroup, Exo-CBX. To add to the confusion, all Exo members have solo music careers and also act in film and television.

Band from Another Planet

Exo was launched with a fantastical backstory more complex than its revolving membership. *Exo* is short for "exoplanets," a term used to define Earth-like planets that circle stars in distant solar systems. Each band member is said to be an alien from a different exoplanet who has a unique superpower. Xiumin purportedly has the power of cryokinesis, the ability to create and manipulate ice by reducing the energy of atoms. Luhan's biography says he is a master of telekinesis—he can move objects with his mind. Lay is a healer who can restore the sick to optimal health—he can cure wounds, broken bones, and diseases. Kai can teleport, while Kris can fly. Other members control water, light, fire, time, and wind. Band members' powers are woven into the plots of music videos, live concert performances, and even commercials the band makes for cell phones, fast food, and other products. The stories behind Exo members have also spawned a mini industry in fan fiction. One website, Asianfanfics, features over 144,000 fictional stories that fans of the band have written about Exo.

Together, the band possesses one superpower that cannot be denied: it has consistently beaten the competition in the race to the top of the charts. Its debut 2012 EP *Mama* (released in two versions, Korean and Mandarin) hit number one on South Korea's Gaon Album Chart, number two on China's Sina Album Chart, and number eight on *Billboard*'s World Albums Chart. Meanwhile, the group's 2013 album *XOXO*, also released in two languages, topped the charts in South Korea and China and hit number three on *Billboard*'s K-Pop Hot 100. Additionally, *XOXO* was the first K-pop album since 2001 to sell over 1 million copies. *XOXO* received numerous awards, including the South Korean Mnet Asian Music Award for Album of the Year.

When Exo released its second EP, *Overdose*, in 2014, the six-song mini album showcased the group as a vocal powerhouse. The title track, "Overdose," was produced by Harvey Mason Jr. and Damon Thomas, American hit makers known as the Underdogs who have worked with Beyoncé, Justin Timberlake, and Pink. As Mason told *Billboard*, "The track is exciting, it's got a lot of energy. It's got some R&B elements, but it's still got a great melody and a big pop hook. . . . It gives [Exo] an opportunity to do what they do."[41] Driven by the hit single, *Overdose* skyrocketed

Exo-K performs in 2014. The band originally consisted of two independent subgroups: Exo-K (pictured) and Exo-M. Exo-K exuded a youthful and innocent image, while Exo-M was for a more mature audience.

to the top of the South Korean charts and even cracked the *Billboard* 200, which charts albums in the United States. When the group announced its first headlining tour, Exo from Exoplanet 1 — the Lost Planet, tickets for the seventy-thousand-seat Seoul arena sold out online in a record-breaking 1.47 seconds.

Lawsuits and Solo Projects

Exo exploded across the K-pop solar system, but all was not well with the band. After the release of *Overdose*, the Chinese-born Canadian singer Kris shocked fans by filing a lawsuit to terminate his exclusive contract with SME. Luhan filed a lawsuit in October 2014, and Tao sued SME in 2015. All the lawsuits addressed the same issues: band members claimed that SME violated their rights by restricting their creative freedom, denying them a fair share of the band's profits, and making them work when they had health problems. The lawsuits were settled in 2016, with the band members agreeing to allow SME to maintain control over their solo careers until 2022.

The lawsuits did little to diminish Exo in the eyes of its fans, and the group continued as a nine-piece band. When *Ex'act* was released in 2016, it was the group's third consecutive studio album to sell more than 1 million copies and the fourth to win the Mnet Asian Music Award for Album of the Year. And like other K-pop idols, various band members pursued solo careers. Baekhyun released a popular single, "Dream," with the South Korean pop singer Suzy. Lay's solo album, *Lose Control*, debuted at number one on the South Korean charts, breaking sales records for a debut album recorded in Chinese. And Chen, Baekhyun,

South Korean Music Television

K-pop fans love to watch their favorite idols perform live, and the existence of numerous South Korean television shows dedicated to music is yet another way that K-pop bands create a loyal following. Those who live in South Korea can find a steady stream of live performances on six television music shows that each air one day of the week, except for Monday: SBS's *Inkigayo*, MBC's *Show! Music Core*, KBS's *Music Bank*, Mnet's *M Countdown*, MBC Music's *Show Champion*, and MTV's *The Show*.

K-pop acts often appear on the shows to promote their latest records. Those making the rounds sometimes appear on each show every day for a month. As music journalist Caitlin Kelley explains, "The constant exposure offered by these music shows is the bread and butter of many acts' marketing in an oversaturated field."

However, appearing on the shows means that band members must follow grueling schedules that require them to prepare, rehearse, and shoot each episode. The physical and mental stress has led to health issues for some performers; in 2016 three members of Exo sued their production company because they were forced to work when sick. But the benefits are too great to ignore. Each day the shows have contests that allow fans to vote for their favorite performers.

Caitlin Kelley, "How Korean Music Shows Diverged from MTV and Became the Epicenter of K-Pop Fan Culture," *Billboard*, September 9, 2017. www.billboard.com.

and Xiumin combined the first letters of their name to create the subgroup Exo-CBX, which released several hit EPs, including the seven-song *Blooming Days*, which featured one tune about each day of the week. The record was an international success, hitting number one on the iTunes charts in places not usually associated with K-pop, including Norway, Greece, Russia, the Philippines, Saudi Arabia, India, and Israel.

All-Time Best Sellers

By the time Exo returned to the studio in 2017 to record its fourth studio album, *The War*, the band was an international sensation. The band's third tour, Exo Planet #3—The EXO'rDIUM, landed Exo in the United States for the first time, with the band playing in Newark, New Jersey, and Los Angeles. The tour also hit Mexico, Japan, and Thailand, where the group sold twenty-four thousand tickets in three minutes.

Shortly before *The War* was released, Exo opened its first official Twitter account, which generated over 11 million tweets about the band within days. The group was the first K-pop act to use Twitter's Instant Unlock feature, which allows registered users to access video teasers and other content. At the end of the year, Twitter reported that Exo was the most followed celebrity to join Twitter in 2017. The group's hit single "Ko Ko Bop" from *The War* was the most tweeted-about song of the year.

In February 2018 Exo played at the closing ceremonies of the Winter Olympics in South Korea. The performance attracted international attention, and when Exo's next album, *Don't Mess Up My Tempo*, was released later that year, it sold over 1.9 million copies. This brought Exo's total albums sales to more than 10 million, making the group the best-selling musical act in South Korean history. *Don't Mess Up My Tempo* was also the first Exo release to debut in the top twenty on the *Billboard* 200. Exo might not be from another planet. But with its superpowers aimed at performing knife-sharp dance routines and turning musical notes into million-selling records, the group has conquered the hearts of millions of fans on planet Earth.

GOT7 Dreams Big

In 2014 JYP Entertainment created its own version of Exo when it pulled together seven members from various Asian nations to form GOT7. JB, Junior (Jinyoung), Youngjae, and Yugyeom are the South Koreans in the group; Mark is an American-born Taiwanese; Jackson hails from Hong Kong; and BamBam is from Thailand.

GOT7 combines rapping, layered harmonies, and soulful R&B with skillfully orchestrated dance moves. K-pop reviewer Julie Jackson describes the band in the following terms: "Looking young, hip and full of energy, GOT7 is a performance-heavy boy band emphasizing gravity-defying B-boy [breakdance] and martial arts–influenced dance moves."[42] The martial arts influence, also known as tricking, incorporates flips, spins, twists, and body corkscrews worthy of a gold medal gymnast.

> "Looking young, hip and full of energy, GOT7 is a performance-heavy boy band emphasizing gravity-defying B-boy [breakdance] and martial arts–influenced dance moves."[42]
>
> —Julie Jackson, K-pop reviewer

GOT7 made its official debut in January 2014 performing the hip-hop song "Girls, Girls, Girls" on *M Countdown*, one of South Korea's six music television shows. The video, which was released simultaneously, exceeded 1 million views on YouTube within two days and ranked as the number one most viewed video in the United States that month. "Girls, Girls, Girls" was the lead track on GOT7's first EP, *Got It?*, which shot to number one on *Billboard*'s World Albums Chart and number two on the Gaon Album Chart. The EP was also popular in Japan.

GOT7 cemented its popularity with the 2014 EP *Got Love*, followed by its first full-length album, *Identify*, which peaked at number four on *Billboard*'s World Digital Songs chart. In 2015 band members increased their visibility by starring in a web fantasy romance drama called *Dream Knight*. The twelve episodes follow a girl who shares her dreams, love, and friendship with a group of mysterious strangers, played by band members. *Dream Knight* amassed over 100 million views, won several South Korean video awards, and was the first web series to be released on DVD.

GOT7 continued to build its following in Japan, releasing several Japanese singles and an entire full-length Japanese studio album called *Moriagatteyo* in 2015. And the group's rising status was confirmed by a host of honors from various entertainment entities, including Best New Artist at the Golden Disk Awards, Best Korean Newcomer at YinYue V Chart Awards, and Most Promising Newcomer Award at the Top Chinese Music Festival.

In 2016 GOT7 expanded its international appeal. The track "Fly" from the group's fifth EP, *Flight Log: Departure*, charted at number forty-five on *Billboard*'s Artist 100. This made GOT7 the first South Korean act to hit that chart since Psy released

GOT7 performs in 2016. Formed in 2014, the K-pop band combines rapping, layered harmonies, and soulful R&B with skillfully orchestrated dance moves.

"Gangnam Style" in 2012. The band launched its Fly Tour in 2016, hitting cities in Singapore, China, Thailand, and Japan. GOT7 also played in the United States for the first time, performing in New York City, Chicago, Dallas, Atlanta, and Los Angeles. Between shows the boys held fan meetings for dedicated followers who call themselves IGot7 or Ahgase. American fans were thrilled to be able to converse with GOT7's four English-speaking members, BamBam, Jackson, Jinyoung, and Mark.

By the time GOT7 launched its 2018 Eyes on You World Tour, the group had grown into one of the world's most prominent K-pop boy bands. After kicking off the tour in Seoul, the band traveled to Thailand, Russia, Germany, and France. GOT7 met with fans and performed in Mexico City, Toronto, and Houston.

The New Language of Pop

Until recently, musical acts that wanted to achieve success in the United States were required to perform in English. To sing in any another language consigned the act to second-tier status. The music would simply not be played on American radio and would only appear on foreign music charts.

K-pop has changed all that, however. Each year, an increasing number of songs and albums that appear on *Billboard*'s American music charts are sung mostly in Korean. For example, BTS's *Love Yourself: Tear*, topped the album charts despite the fact that it features lyrics that most Westerners do not understand. Indeed, with Korean-language music and videos by Exo, Red Velvet, BTS, and BlackPink setting streaming records and garnering billions of hits on YouTube, it seems that language is no barrier when it comes to developing a worldwide fan base.

Anyone who has been to an Exo or Red Velvet concert knows that it is not necessary to understand Korean to love the harmonies, dancing, and spectacular light shows. As more Americans find common ground listening to their favorite K-pop idols, they are finding that a shared love of music and cultural diversity can help them transcend barriers imposed by language.

Nothing better demonstrated GOT7's growing popularity than the fact that it sold out the seventeen-thousand-seat Barclays Center arena in New York City. When GOT7 played New York two years earlier, it was barely able to fill the twenty-one-hundred-seat PlayStation Theater in Times Square.

The American leg of the Eyes on You World Tour ended at the Los Angeles Forum. K-pop journalist Rosan Powierza describes the scene: "It was a hot Friday night, but thousands of fans spent two-and-a-half hours screaming at the top of their lungs, laughing, crying, singing, and dancing to their beloved group's performances."[43]

While GOT7 expanded its fan base, it was also growing creatively. Several members of the group contributed to the lyrics and music on GOT7's eighth EP, *Eyes on You* (2018). The track "Look," cowritten by JB, topped the international music charts and went on to become the band's most successful song. As 2019 got underway, GOT7 continued to aim for major success in the United States. "It's just beginning in America for K-pop culture," says BamBam. "[I'm] gonna dream big . . . [and] later on I hope another K-pop artist, when they come to America, they can get some energy from us."[44]

> "It's just beginning in America for K-pop culture."[44]
>
> —BamBam, GOT7 singer

Red Velvet's Girl Crush

While boy bands like GOT7 and Exo were selling out shows and winning awards in the United States, girl groups seemed to be receiving less attention. But that equation began to change, thanks to the five members of Red Velvet: Joy, Yeri, Irene, Seulgi, and Wendy. When Red Velvet kicked off its five-city Redmare in USA tour in 2019, it was the first K-pop girl group to tour America since 2016. Red Velvet sold out its shows in Dallas, Miami, Chicago, and Newark within minutes. The group had to add a second show in Los Angeles to meet the huge demand for tickets, prompting Seulgi to comment: "[I] really, really felt pride that the LA show sold out within a minute. It's really awesome. It kind of makes [me] feel like the group should work harder to give back to the fans for all the love [we've] received."[45]

Like some other K-pop acts, Red Velvet has an overarching theme that guides the band's output. "Red" and "velvet" define two distinct images and musical styles. The red part of the band is associated with a bright, bubbly image and catchy pop numbers like "Dumb Dumb" (2015) and "Red Flavor" (2017). When the band is projecting its velvet side, however, it has a softer, more mature image, associated with slower, sultry R&B-flavored songs like "Automatic" and "Bad Boy," which were both released in 2015.

> "[I] really, really felt pride that the LA show sold out within a minute. It's really awesome. It kind of makes [me] feel like the group should work harder to give back to the fans."[45]
>
> —Seulgi, Red Velvet singer

Red Velvet debuted as a four-member group in 2014 with the single "Happiness," a red-themed song with a catchy melody and exhilarating dance beat. "Happiness" was the first K-pop girl group single to debut on *Billboard*'s World Digital Songs chart, peaking at number four. With its humorous animation and joyous choreography, the video swiftly collected 2 million hits on YouTube and went on to garner 82 million views by 2019. The band followed up its initial success with a velvet-themed song, "Natural," which featured a video choreographed by Irene and Seulgi.

Yeri joined Red Velvet in 2015, adding her vocals to the group's first EP, *Ice Cream Cake*. This was followed up by the band's first full-length album, *The Red*, which debuted at number one on South Korea's Gaon Album Chart and *Billboard*'s World Albums Chart. *Billboard* also included *The Red* on its list of 10 Best K-Pop Albums of 2015. Red Velvet followed up with an EP, *The*

When Red Velvet kicked off its five-city US tour in 2019, it was the first K-pop girl group to tour the United States since 2016. Red Velvet sold out shows in Dallas, Miami, Chicago, and Newark within minutes.

Velvet (2016), which featured suave R&B songs that highlighted the other side of the band's image.

Red Velvet followed the trajectory of other K-pop bands shooting for the stars. In 2017 it released several EPs and a full-length album, with videos that topped the charts and attracted millions of views. As the group's popularity grew, it performed live concerts in Japan, South Korea, and elsewhere. In addition to the usual statistics surrounding downloads and ticket sales, Red Velvet attracted attention for creating music that showcased confident, empowered women. This made Red Velvet one of the most visible expressions of the K-pop concept known as girl crush. Music journalist Caitlin Kelley describes the girl crush phenomenon in the following way: "There are the usual [clothing] signifiers: sports jerseys, fishnets, menswear, Doc Martens [boots] and dark color schemes. Basically, anything that conveys the image of ferocity, stepping outside the expectations of hyperfemininity."[46]

While K-pop boy bands tend to attract loyal female fans, most girl groups have male followers. Even so, around three-quarters of Red Velvet fans are females who are inspired by songs like "RBB (Really Bad Boy)." The video portrays a bad boy as a werewolf-like monster that threatens women, who remain unafraid. Joy explains female fans' appreciation of the band in the following way: "If you listen to a lot of Red Velvet songs, they're about being confident, bold, being yourself. So [I] think that's kind of why that message—that kind of confident message—is what appeals to female fans in particular."[47]

In 2018 Red Velvet released the eight-track EP *Summer Magic*. The lead single, "Power Up," quickly topped all five of Korea's music charts, named Bugs, Melon, Soribada, Monkey3, and Dosirak. The act of hitting number one on all five charts is called a perfect all-kill, or PAK.

Circling the Globe

Red Velvet, Exo, and GOT7 are, along with K-pop groups like BTS and BlackPink, making historic inroads in the United States. Other up-and-coming girl groups like Twice and GFriend—along with boy bands Shinee, Monsta X, and Astro—are helping make

K-pop more popular than ever on the international stage. Numerous bands that rap and sing in Korean are planning multicity tours in the United States, and many are also beginning to visit cities in Europe, the Middle East, and South America. Fans are taking part in this burgeoning global movement—K-pop as a topic generated over 5.3 billion tweets in 2018.

From Seoul to Los Angeles, New York, London, Dubai, and beyond, K-pop music is circling the globe at the speed of light. As this unique sound travels from entertainment companies to fans via billions of cell phones, televisions, and computers, K-pop is changing the musical world. Indeed, music, dance, fashion, and even the meaning of music fandom will never be the same.

${\mathcal{S}}$OURCE NOTES

Introduction: A Worldwide Explosion

1. Amy X. Wang, "How K-Pop Conquered the West," *Rolling Stone*, August 21, 2018. www.rollingstone.com.
2. Wang, "How K-Pop Conquered the West."
3. Quoted in Wang, "How K-Pop Conquered the West."
4. Quoted in Wang, "How K-Pop Conquered the West."
5. Brian O'Flynn, "The K-Pop Phenomenon: 'It's Pop Music on Crack,'" *Irish Times*, October 27, 2018. www.irishtimes.com.

Chapter One: Origins of K-Pop

6. Suk-Young Kim, *K-Pop Live: Fans, Idols, and Multimedia Performance*. Stanford, CA: Stanford University Press, 2018, p. 7.
7. Simon Stawski and Martina Stawski, "Jumping BoAs and Kpop Fan Groups," Eat Your Kimchi, October 27, 2010. www.eatyourkimchi.com.
8. Quoted in Robert Michael Poole, "A K-Pop Sensation Plays Letterman," *Scene Asia* (blog), *Wall Street Journal*, January 31, 2012. http://blogs.wsj.com.

Chapter Two: K-Pop Musicians of Influence

9. Quoted in Stevie Chick, "Shin Joong Hyun: South Korea's Psychedelic Mimic Turned Master," *Guardian* (Manchester), September 15, 2011. www.theguardian.com.
10. Hannah Waitt, "The History of Kpop, Chapter 3: Seo Taiji and the Boys," MoonROK, July 7, 2017. www.moonrok.com.
11. Roald Maliangkay, "Hard Acts to Follow: Seo Taeji and the Boys," University of California, Irvine, 2011. www.humanities.uci.edu.

12. Quoted in Mark James Russell, *Pop Goes Korea*. Berkeley, CA: Stone Bridge, 2008, p. 144.
13. Russell, *Pop Goes Korea*, p. 146.
14. Quoted in Deborah Sontag, "The Ambassador," *New York Times*, January 29, 2006. www.nytimes.com.
15. Quoted in Sontag, "The Ambassador."
16. Quoted in Sontag, "The Ambassador."
17. Quoted in Sontag, "The Ambassador."
18. Quoted in Patrick Doyle, "Things You Didn't Know About Psy," *Rolling Stone*, November 22, 2012, p. 24.
19. Quoted in Brian Hiatt, "Can Psy Move Past 'Gangnam Style'?," *Rolling Stone*, December 6, 2012, p. 22.
20. Quoted in Roger Hamilton, "6 Trips to Get to Gangnam 1 Billion Views," NextUpAsia, February 13, 2013. www.nextup asia.com.
21. Quoted in Hiatt, "Can Psy Move Past 'Gangnam Style'?," p. 22.

Chapter Three: Creating a Following

22. Quoted in Wendy Lee, "Coachella in Times Square," *Los Angeles Times*, April 10, 2019, p. C3.
23. Rowena Chandler, "K-Pop on YouTube: How the Platform Has Made it Global," Artifice, August 17, 2016. https://the -artifice.com.
24. Chandler, "K-Pop on YouTube."
25. Daphne Kwong, "Singing the Praises of K-Pop's BTS," *Los Angeles Times*, April 7, 2019, p. E2.
26. Quoted in Caitlin Kelley, "BTS' 11 Most Socially Conscious Songs Before 'Go Go,'" *Billboard*, September 18, 2018. www.billboard.com.
27. Quoted in Giovanna Trabasso, "BTS Is Tackling Problems That Are Taboo," Affinity Magazine, May 29, 2016. http://af finitymagazine.us.

28. Aja Romano, "BTS, the Band That Changed K-Pop, Explained," Vox, September 26, 2018. www.vox.com.

29. Quoted in Kevin Sprague, "K-Pop Band Uses Fan Reaction Videos as a Promotional Tool," UCLA Center for Korean Studies, March 14, 2018. www.international.ucla.edu.

30. Jade Hookham, "BTS Is a Social Media Success Story," Study Breaks, May 11, 2018. https://studybreaks.com.

31. E. Alex Jung, "40,000 BTS Fans Can't Be Wrong," Vulture, October 10, 2018. www.vulture.com.

32. Jung, "40,000 BTS Fans Can't Be Wrong."

33. Quoted in Claire Dodson, "BTS's New Album 'Love Yourself: Tear' Is Out, and the BTS Army Is Already Picking Favorites," Teen Vogue, May 18, 2018. www.teenvogue.com.

34. Quoted in Bea Midesya, "BTS Breaks Records and Makes History," Pepperdine University Graphic, October 2, 2017. https://pepperdine-graphic.com.

35. Quoted in Emily Blake, "The Strength of K-Pop Fandom, by the Numbers," Forbes, April 4, 2018. www.forbes.com.

36. Quoted in Blake, "The Strength of K-Pop Fandom, by the Numbers."

37. Jung, "40,000 BTS Fans Can't Be Wrong."

38. Jung, "40,000 BTS Fans Can't Be Wrong."

39. Jung, "40,000 BTS Fans Can't Be Wrong."

Chapter Four: K-Pop's Reigning Royalty

40. Quoted in Around the O, "K-Pop Could Be America's Next Musical Invasion, Prof Writes," June 27, 2018. https://around.uoregon.edu.

41. Quoted in Jeff Benjamin, "The Underdogs Talk EXO's 'Overdose,' Tease 'Game-Changing' K-Pop Records: Exclusive," Billboard, April 25, 2014. www.billboard.com.

42. Julie Jackson, "GOT7 Returning with New EP," Korea Herald, June 25, 2014. www.koreaherald.com.

43. Rosan Powierza, "GOT7 2018 World Tour 'EYES ON YOU' Captivates North America!," KPOP Channel.tv, July 13, 2018. www.kpopchannel.tv.

44. Quoted in Tamar Herman, "Boy Band GOT7 Talk Making Their Own Way Amid Growing Stateside Interest in K-Pop," *Forbes*, July 18, 2018. www.forbes.com.

45. Quoted in Alexis Hodoyan-Gastelum, "Red Velvet Is the Girl Group K-Pop Fangirls Have Been Waiting For," *OC Weekly*, February 5, 2019. https://ocweekly.com.

46. Caitlin Kelley, "How 'Girl Crush' Hooked Female Fans and Grappled with Feminism as K-Pop Went Global in 2018," *Billboard*, December 27, 2018. www.billboard.com.

47. Quoted in Hodoyan-Gastelum, "Red Velvet Is the Girl Group K-Pop Fangirls Have Been Waiting For."

$\mathcal{F}$OR FURTHER RESEARCH

Books

Annika Chung, *All About K-Pop: Inside Stories Behind K-Pop's Rise to Global Fandom*. Vancouver, Canada: Coal Harbour, 2018.

Fandom Media, ed., *KPOP EXO Quiz Book: 123 Fun Facts Trivia Questions About the Hottest K-Pop Band*. Denver: New Ampersand, 2018.

Woosung Kang, *The Kpop Dictionary: 500 Essential Korean Slang Words and Phrases Every Kpop Fan Must Know*. Denver: New Ampersand, 2016.

Dianne Pineda-Kim, *K-Pop Style: Fashion, Skin-Care, Make-Up, Lifestyle, and More*. New York: Racehorse, 2019.

Katy Sprinkel, *The Big Book of BTS: The Deluxe Unofficial Bangtan Book*. Chicago: Triumph, 2019.

Internet Sources

Emily Blake, "The Strength of K-Pop Fandom, by the Numbers," *Forbes*, April 4, 2018. www.forbes.com.

Rowena Chandler, "K-Pop on YouTube: How the Platform Has Made It Global," Artifice, August 17, 2016. https://the-artifice.com.

Alexis Hodoyan-Gastelum, "Red Velvet Is the Girl Group K-Pop Fangirls Have Been Waiting For," *OC Weekly*, February 5, 2019. https://ocweekly.com.

Caitlin Kelley, "How 'Girl Crush' Hooked Female Fans and Grappled with Feminism as K-Pop Went Global in 2018," *Billboard*, December 27, 2018. www.billboard.com.

Amy Wang, "How K-Pop Conquered the West," *Rolling Stone*, August 21, 2018. www.rollingstone.com.

Websites

Allkpop (www.allkpop.com). Allkpop was launched in 2007 to cover K-pop celebrity gossip, breaking news, and controversies. The site features a number of forums on which fans discuss K-pop, J-pop, Chinese pop music, films, anime, and TV shows.

Amino (https://aminoapps.com). The K-pop section of the Amino website is an immersive experience, with videos, music, public chat rooms, and hundreds of articles focused on K-pop bands and idols. A mobile app with a paid monthly membership is available.

Koreaboo (www.koreaboo.com). Koreaboo is the founder of KCON, and its fan website creates and shares viral Korean pop content in English, with 40 million users in over one hundred countries. The site features K-pop news articles, stories, lists, and fashion and beauty tips.

KPOP Channel.tv (www.kpopchannel.tv). This English-language, Seoul-based website focuses on South Korean music, stars, film, and culture. The site features dozens of K-pop videos, interviews with idols, beauty and fashion sections, and reviews of music, concerts, and TV shows.

Soompi (www.soompi.com). Founded in 1998, Soompi the largest and longest-running English-language website covering South Korean pop culture. With its features on K-pop music, videos, celebrities, food, and fashion, Soompi is the go-to place for dedicated K-pop fans.

INDEX